WE'RE THE CENTER OF THE UNIVERSE!

SCIENCE'S BIGGEST MISTAKES ABOUT ASTRONOMY AND PHYSICS

CHRISTINE ZUCHORA-WALSKE

Publications Company · Minneapolis

Lerner Publications Company
A division of Lerner Publishing Group, Inc.
241 First Avenue North
Minneapolis, MN 55401 USA

For reading levels and more information, look up this title at www.lernerbooks.com.

Main body text set in Avenir LT Pro 12/18.
Typeface provided by Linotype AG.

Library of Congress Cataloging-in-Publication Data

Zuchora-Walske, Christine, author.
    We're the center of the universe! : science's biggest mistakes about astronomy and physics / by Christine Zuchora-Walske.
        pages   cm. — (Science gets it wrong)
    Includes index.
    ISBN 978–1–4677–3663–3 (lib. bdg. : alk. paper)
    ISBN 978–1–4677–4739–4 (eBook)
    1. Astronomy—Juvenile literature. 2. Cosmology—Juvenile literature. 3. Physics—Juvenile literature. 4. Errors, Scientific—Juvenile literature. I. Title. II. Title: We are the center of the universe!
    QB46.Z83 2015
    520—dc23   5191
                                                                    2013045903

Manufactured in the United States of America
1 — DP — 7/15/14

CONTENTS

The whole universe circles around Earth.
The motions of stars and planets affect human lives. The sun is a planet, and creatures live there!

In earlier times, many people believed ideas like these. They were once examples of the best available scientific thinking.

For as long as humans have existed, we've tried to understand the universe. Early humans used simple methods to examine the skies and Earth. They tried to figure out the rules of nature. They asked questions, made observations, and performed tests. These steps became the basis of science. Over time, people developed tools for studying the skies. They made astrolabes, devices that determined the position of objects in the sky. They built telescopes, which magnified distant objects.

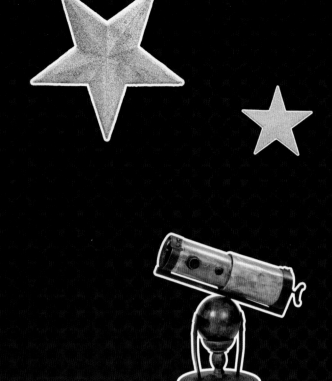

As we improved our scientific knowledge, sometimes we confirmed old ideas. Sometimes we realized we'd been terribly wrong. Oops!

Science is a constant search for new facts. And new facts can reveal problems with old ideas.

So go ahead and laugh at the silly science of the past. But remember: in the future, people might think our scientific ideas are pretty goofy too!

This model of the universe from 1540 shows Earth surrounded by orbiting celestial bodies.

WE'RE THE CENTER OF THE UNIVERSE!

Does your little brother act like the center of the universe? Well, he's not the first. In ancient times, people thought the sun and the stars circled around our planet. This seemed like common sense. After all, anybody could see the sun moving across the sky during the day and the stars moving across the sky at night.

In ancient Egypt, a scientist named Ptolemy put the idea in writing. He explained that Earth stood still while everything else in the universe moved around it. Some ancient scientists disagreed with Ptolemy. But his theory lasted for around twelve hundred years.

Ptolemy

Who spun Ptolemy's idea on its head? It was Polish astronomer Nicolaus Copernicus. He wrote *On the Revolutions of the Celestial Spheres* in 1543. Copernicus said the sun was at the center of the universe. He said that Earth and other heavenly bodies **orbit** the sun.

orbit: to repeatedly move around another object in a curved path

Copernicus's ideas weren't 100 percent correct. The whole universe doesn't move around the sun. Only Earth's **solar system** does. And the sun isn't exactly at the center of the solar system. The planets move in oval paths. But Copernicus pushed science in the right direction.

In the 1600s, Italian scientist Galileo Galilei studied the sky using telescopes. He too said that Earth and the other planets orbit the sun. Galileo's ideas angered leaders of the Christian Church. They said Earth did not move, because that's what was written in the Christian Bible.

However, the world could not ignore the arguments of Copernicus and Galileo for long. More powerful telescopes and other tools showed their ideas to be correct.

BEFORE THE TELESCOPE

Some ancient groups built structures aligned with the skies. For instance, windows were placed so that the sun lit up a certain room only on a certain day of the year. People in ancient Mexico built a pyramid-temple called El Castillo. On the shortest and longest days of the year, one corner of the temple casts a shadow as the sun sets. The shadow looks like a snake slithering down the side of the temple. El Castillo and similar buildings helped people keep track of time and the seasons.

solar system: a star and the collection of planets, moons, and smaller objects that circle the star

THOSE GOOFY WANDERING STARS

You and your dad are walking the dog after dark. A bright light crosses the sky. "Dad! A shooting star!" you say. Your dad explains that the light is actually from the International Space Station. Your shooting star wasn't a star after all. You're learning that objects in the sky aren't always what they seem.

Humans have been learning this lesson for a long time. In ancient times, people looked into the sky and saw the moon and the stars. They also saw the planets Mercury, Venus, Mars, Jupiter, and Saturn. These five planets are close enough to be seen with the naked eye.

The planets reflect the sun's light. They appear to be shining. Since they look much like all the other tiny lights in the sky, ancient people thought they were stars.

These five "stars" acted a little goofy, though. All the other stars crossed the sky together from east to west. But the goofy stars moved east instead of west. They also moved along wavy, looping paths. The ancient Greeks called them *planetes asteres,* or "wandering stars."

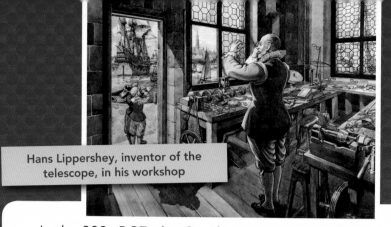

Hans Lippershey, inventor of the telescope, in his workshop

In the 300s BCE, the Greek **astronomer** Eudoxus tried to explain the movement of stars. He said that Earth sat at the center of the universe. He believed that many clear shells, one inside the other, surrounded Earth. He said the shells spun around Earth, carrying objects in the sky with them. He thought the outermost shell, moving east to west, carried the regular stars. Inside that, he said, other shells carried the "wandering stars," the sun, and the moon.

Ptolemy and Copernicus also examined the wandering stars. Ptolemy said that while each one moved around Earth, it also moved in smaller circles, called epicycles. Copernicus disagreed. He said the loopy movements were an optical illusion. It occurred when a fast, wandering star moved past a slower one. When this happened, the slower one appeared to be moving backward.

Copernicus

A Dutch lens maker named Hans Lippershey invented the telescope in 1608. With telescopes, astronomers could see that "wandering stars" are not stars at all. They are planets. They are lit by the sun, which makes them shine in the night sky. And Copernicus was correct: the planets' loopy movements are an optical illusion.

astronomer: a scientist who studies the universe and the objects in it

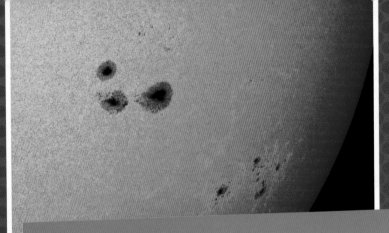

HOT TIMES ON PLANET SUN

In the 1837 science-fiction book *Journeys into the Moon, Several Planets and the Sun,* a woman travels to various places in our solar system. She explains, "The climate in the sun is more than refreshingly and pleasantly warm; we inhabitants of the earth believe the sun to be a real ball of fire, which he by no means is."

The story goes on to tell about people living on the sun. Sound ridiculous? It didn't back then. Even famous British astronomer William Herschel (1738–1822) thought that creatures lived on the sun.

During Herschel's lifetime, scientists were just learning about the sun. Looking through telescopes, they saw that the sun was a glowing ball with some dark spots. Herschel wrote that the spots were holes in the sun's **atmosphere**. Below the atmosphere, he

William Herschel

atmosphere: a layer of gases surrounding a planet or other body in space

wrote, the sun had a cool dark surface. He thought the sun was a planet like all the others.

Eventually, other scientists chipped away at Herschel's ideas. In 1807 British scientist Thomas Young said that nothing could live on the sun because its **gravity** was too powerful. In 1821, Scottish scientist David Brewster

A NEW PLANET

Using a telescope, William Herschel discovered the planet Uranus *(right)* in 1781. This was the first discovery of a planet in thousands of years. Humans had known about Mercury, Venus, Mars, Jupiter, and Saturn since ancient times. These planets are visible in the night sky without a telescope.

said that the sun was too hot for living things. By the late 1800s, scientists knew that stars were giant balls of burning gases. They realized that the sun was a star.

It's fun to imagine creatures living on the sun. But modern scientists say that life is possible only in certain places. To support life, a place must have liquid water. It must have certain chemicals, such as carbon, hydrogen, oxygen, and nitrogen. It needs a thick atmosphere to protect living things from harmful energy from space. It also must not be too hot or too cold. Earth is the only place in the solar system that meets these requirements.

gravity: a force that makes every object pull on every other object. Larger, denser objects pull more than smaller, airier ones. This pull is greatest on objects nearby.

BEWARE THE MARTIAN HORDES!

In the 1898 book *War of the Worlds*, H. G. Wells described a Martian:

> Those who have never seen a living Martian can scarcely imagine the strange horror of its appearance. The peculiar V-shaped mouth with its pointed upper lip . . . the Gorgon groups of tentacles . . . the immense eyes— were . . . monstrous . . . unspeakably nasty.

Do creatures really live on Mars? No. But for many years, scientists thought they did.

In the 1600s and the 1700s, scientists studied Mars through telescopes. From 1777 to 1783, William Herschel observed Mars carefully. He wrote about its shape, size, and thin atmosphere. He claimed that Mars's dark areas were oceans and its light areas were land. He said that the Martians living there "probably enjoy a situation similar to our own."

Planet Mars

Using observations made through telescopes, Giovanni Schiaparelli made this map of Mars.

Later in the 1800s, Italian astronomer Giovanni Schiaparelli spotted streaks on the Martian surface. He called them *canali,* or channels.

This discovery thrilled US astronomer Percival Lowell. Perhaps living things had built the channels, he thought. Lowell built an **observatory** in Flagstaff, Arizona. This research center had a powerful telescope. From there, Lowell studied Mars. In 1894, he declared that the streaks on Mars were canals for water. He said they had been cut by living beings.

Belief in life on Mars fizzled in the 1960s. That's when humans began sending spacecraft to explore the solar system. First, people sent spacecraft to orbit Mars. The orbiters took pictures of Mars from out in space. Later, people sent rovers to Mars. These small, remote-controlled carts traveled over the Martian surface. The rovers took close-up photos of Mars, tested Mars rocks, and mapped the planet.

The orbiters and the rovers didn't find evidence of living things, but scientists think that Mars might have been home to living things millions or billions of years ago. Until scientists find definite proof of life on Mars, tales of Martians will remain in the fiction section of the library.

observatory: a place used for studying the sun, moon, stars, planets, and other celestial bodies. Observatories have powerful telescopes and other machines.

Arrows in these two photos taken in 1938 show the newly discovered planet of Pluto.

POOR LITTLE PLUTO

Pluto has always been the underdog of our solar system. Not only was it thought to be the smallest planet, it was also the farthest from the sun. To make matters worse, in 2006, scientists declared that Pluto wasn't a planet at all!

If Pluto's not a planet, then what is it? To answer this question, it helps to travel back in time to 1781, when Uranus was discovered. While observing Uranus with telescopes, astronomers noticed a wobble in its orbit. If pulled only by the gravity of the sun and the six inner planets, Uranus shouldn't wobble. So scientists said that another planet, farther out, must be pulling on Uranus.

In 1846, astronomers located Neptune. Neptune's pull explained some of Uranus's wobble but not all of it. And scientists saw that Neptune was wobbly too. They guessed that yet another planet lay beyond Neptune. They called it Planet X.

In 1930, US astronomer Clyde Tombaugh found Planet X. He compared photos of the same region of the night sky taken two weeks apart. Planet X was in different positions in those photos. That meant it was a moving object. Scientists renamed the object Pluto, after the Roman god of the dead.

Clyde Tombaugh

In the late 1900s, scientists studied Pluto with powerful telescopes. They figured out it was half the size of the tiny planet of Mercury. They discovered that Pluto has several moons. They also learned that about seventy thousand other objects travel through the solar system at about the same distance from the sun as Pluto. Many of these objects are as big as Pluto. Their neighborhood is called the Kuiper Belt.

After discovering the Kuiper Belt, astronomers made a new definition of a planet. To be a planet, an object must orbit the sun; have enough gravity to pull itself into a ball; and orbit on its own, without other objects nearby, except its moons.

Pluto broke the last rule. Thousands of objects cluttered Pluto's orbit. So Pluto was reclassified as a dwarf planet. That is what it really is. It's not actually a planet at all.

In 2006, the US space program launched the *New Horizons* spacecraft to Pluto. The craft is due to arrive in July 2015. It will take the first-ever close-up pictures of Pluto. Then we'll learn even more about the dwarf planet!

An illustration of the solar system shows the outer rocky ring called the Kuiper Belt.

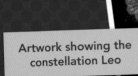

Artwork showing the constellation Leo

Do you read your horoscope in the newspaper or online each day? If so, you're dabbling in astrology. Astrology is the practice of studying the stars, the planets, the sun, the moon, and other heavenly objects to learn about human events. An astrologer creates a horoscope, a prediction for the future. Horoscopes are usually based on the position of heavenly bodies at the time of someone's birth.

To many modern people, astrology seems silly. To our ancestors, however, astrology offered a way to make sense of a complicated world.

Stars are spaced unevenly in Earth's sky. Many constellations, or groups of stars, seem to form pictures. When ancient people saw pictures in the stars, they named the images they saw. Ancient constellations include Pisces, which looks like a fish, and Leo, which resembles a lion.

Medieval astrologers *(top)* examine the skies.

Ancient people thought that constellations could affect humans. For instance, they thought a fish-shaped constellation affected water on Earth.

Thousands of years ago, astrology was considered a serious science. Ptolemy said that the movement

Johannes Kepler

of the planets created an ever-changing situation on Earth. He said all Earth's creatures, including people, were sensitive to the changes. The ancient Chinese also believed in astrology. They said the positions of the planets, the sun, the moon, and the comets at the time of a person's birth determined his or her destiny.

In the 1600s, telescopes gave people a better view of the night sky. This sparked an explosion of scientific observations and measurements. Once humans knew more about the universe, they relied less on astrology to answer their questions.

In modern times, most people see astrology as superstition. In his 1980 TV series *Cosmos*, astronomer Carl Sagan explained that heavenly bodies can't influence our lives. They are simply too far away for their light or gravity to affect us.

Two photos taken at the same place about six hours apart show both high *(left)* and low *(right)* tides.

AS EARTH MOVES, THE OCEANS SLOSH

In ancient times, people who lived by the seashore sometimes observed the tides. Every day, they saw the sea rise to a peak level, or high tide. About six hours later, they saw the water fall to low tide. Six hours after that, the water rose again. The cycle continued day after day. But no one knew why.

In 1595, Galileo was riding on a barge. It carried tanks of freshwater to Venice, Italy. Galileo noticed that as the barge sped up, slowed down, or turned, the water sloshed around in the tanks. This motion gave him an idea.

Galileo knew that Earth spun around once per day and also orbited the sun. He thought these motions made the oceans on Earth slosh about, just like the water on the barge.

In 1609, German astronomer Johannes Kepler offered a different explanation. Kepler believed that the moon caused

tides: the rise and fall of seawater on Earth caused primarily by the moon's gravity

The moon's gravity has a strong pull on Earth's oceans.

tides, but he didn't know how. Galileo dismissed Kepler's idea. He thought it was as silly as astrology.

In 1616, Galileo explained his idea in a paper called "Treatise on the Tides." He repeated it in his 1632 book *Dialogue Concerning the Two Chief World Systems.* Galileo's tide theory lived on for decades after his death in 1642.

Galileo was wrong about Earth's tides. They are not caused by the motions of Earth. They are mostly caused by the moon's gravity pulling on Earth's oceans. In 1687, English scientist Isaac Newton published his ideas about gravity. Scientists soon figured out that Kepler had been right. The moon creates most of the tides on Earth.

The sun's gravity also creates tides on Earth, but because the sun is so far away, these tides are much weaker than those created by the moon. The moon

Isaac Newton

travels around Earth in an oval orbit, so sometimes the moon is farther away from Earth than other times. When the moon is closest to Earth, tides are strongest.

The famous Bayeux Tapestry, created in England in the late 1000s CE, shows Halley's comet streaking through the sky.

DON'T GET HIT BY A COMET!

It was an ordinary evening in ancient Babylon. Farmers headed home after tending their fields. Women prepared and served foods. As they went about their business, people glanced up at the sky. They saw an unfamiliar light. It looked like a big, bright star with a tail. People were afraid. They'd seen a comet, and comets were never good.

In earlier centuries, humans had no idea what comets were. Most people thought comets were bad omens—signs of future disaster. People also thought comets were dangerous. They worried that a comet might strike Earth.

Aristotle, an ancient Greek thinker, saw that most heavenly bodies moved in predictable ways. But comets were random and unpredictable. So Aristotle thought they weren't part of the heavens. Instead, he believed that comets came from Earth's atmosphere, just as lightning does. No one argued with this idea for more than a thousand years.

Then, in 1577, Danish astronomer Tycho Brahe carefully

studied a comet. By looking at it from different angles, he saw that the comet was farther from Earth than the moon was.

This illustration shows a comet streaking across the sky in 1577.

In 1687, Isaac Newton proposed that comets orbited the sun, just as the planets did. British astronomer Edmond Halley studied records of past comets. He also observed a comet in 1682. He compared its path to that of earlier comets. It turned out that the paths of comets in 1531, 1607, and 1682 were all the same. Halley guessed that it was the same comet, circling the sun once about every seventy-six years. He predicted it would pass Earth again in 1758. He was right. Astronomers named it Halley's comet.

Edmond Halley

Modern scientists have studied comets through powerful telescopes. They have even sent spacecraft to study comets up close. Scientists have tracked many comets and know how long they take to orbit the sun.

A comet is like a big, dirty snowball. The center is made of dust and rocks held together by frozen water and gases. As a comet nears the sun, it heats up. The ice melts and the gases escape, creating a glowing cloud around the comet. Some of this gas forms a long tail behind the comet.

Since we know what comets are, they don't scare us anymore. People no longer run and hide when a comet comes around.

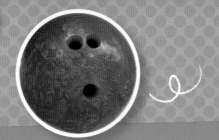

SMACKDOWN! GOLF BALL VERSUS BOWLING BALL

Suppose you dropped a golf ball and a bowling ball out a second-story window. Which one would hit the ground first?

Aristotle believed that the heavier an object was, the faster it would fall. So Aristotle would have said that your bowling ball would hit the ground first. But Aristotle didn't test this idea.

Then along came Galileo. He was an experimenter. He tested every idea that interested him. Legend says that in the late 1500s, Galileo climbed to the top of Italy's Leaning Tower of Pisa. According to the story, he dropped a large iron cannonball and a small iron musket ball at the same time, and the balls hit the ground at nearly the same time. This experiment, if it really took place, disproved Aristotle's idea that heavier objects fall faster.

According to legend, Galileo dropped a musket ball and a cannonball to learn about gravity.

Galileo went on to explain falling objects in great detail. He said that not all objects fall at the same speed. Some objects fall more slowly than others because of **friction**. That is, as objects fall, they rub against gases in the air. This rubbing slows the falling objects. Galileo said that friction affects lighter objects more strongly than heavier objects. Galileo wished he could do his experiment in a vacuum, a place without any air to create friction. In a vacuum, he said, *any* two objects dropped from the same height would hit the ground at the same time.

Four centuries later, scientists were able to test Galileo's theory. In 1971, astronaut David Scott visited the moon. He dropped a feather and a hammer to the moon's surface at the same time. The moon has no atmosphere, so there was no air to slow the falling objects. Just as Galileo had predicted, both items hit the dirt at the exact same time!

Astronaut David Scott holds a hammer in his right hand and a feather in his left.

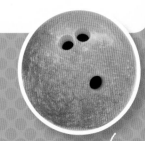

friction: the rubbing of one object or substance against another. Friction slows down moving objects.

EVERYTHING IS MADE OF EARTH, AIR, FIRE, AND WATER

Let's say you're a scientist in ancient times. You want to figure out what nature is made of. You focus on the **matter** around you. You feel the air and breathe it in. You cup your hand in water and take a drink. You light a fire. You study a rock. Then you hammer it into bits. You examine the bits.

After careful study, you conclude that even if you could divide a breath of air, a handful of water, a flame, or a rock forever, the particles would still be air, water, fire, or rock. This is what most ancient Greek scholars believed. They thought that all matter was made of four basic elements—fire, air, earth, and water. They said these elements could be divided endlessly into tinier and tinier particles of fire, air, earth, and water.

A scholar named Democritus disagreed. In the 400s BCE, he developed an idea called atomic theory. He said that if you divided matter into smaller and smaller pieces, eventually you would end

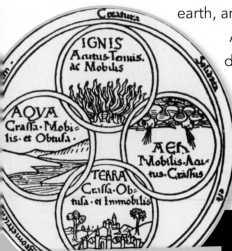

An illustration from the 1500s shows the world as being made of four elements (*clockwise from top*): fire, air, earth, and water.

matter: the substance

up with tiny particles called atoms. He said these couldn't be divided any further.

Other Greek thinkers disagreed. Aristotle thought atomic theory was too simple to explain the complex universe. After Aristotle, most scientists continued to think that earth, air, fire, and water were the most basic particles of matter.

In the 1600s, Irish chemist Robert Boyle experimented with gases and metals. His experiments showed that earth, air, fire, and water were not the most basic particles. Boyle agreed with Democritus that atoms were the basic units of matter. John Dalton, a British chemist, said that different kinds of atoms combined to create different kinds of substances. For instance, he said that water is made from a combination of hydrogen and oxygen atoms. In the 1700s, scientists identified many elements, or substances that contain only one kind of atom. These are the building blocks of matter.

Modern scientists have studied atoms closely. They know that atoms are made up of even smaller particles. And atoms can be split— with some difficulty. But Democritus had the basics right.

John Dalton

NO MATTER?
NO LIGHT

Light is both obvious and mysterious. It surrounds us every day, brightening our world. Even so, scientists have had a hard time understanding it.

Early scientists pondered how we see. The ancient Greeks realized that light travels in rays, or straight lines. The Middle Eastern mathematician Alhazen, who lived in the 900s and 1000s, figured out that we see things when light bounces off objects and into our eyes.

In 1690, Dutch astronomer Christiaan Huygens suggested that light was like sound. Sound begins when an object vibrates. That makes the air or other matter (such as water) around the object vibrate. The vibrating matter travels to our ears in waves.

Huygens believed that light worked the same way. He said a substance called ether

Alhazen

filled the empty space between objects. He said that light formed when an object created wavelike vibrations in ether. When the vibrating ether met someone's eye, that person saw the object.

Isaac Newton disagreed with Huygens. In 1704, Newton said that light was made of streams of tiny, fast-moving particles. He said that light traveled in straight lines, not waves.

Isaac Newton used a prism to split light into bands of color.

Huygens and Newton were both wrong. And they were both right too. A ray of light acts like a wave *and* like a stream of particles.

Light is made up of bundles of energy called photons. Imagine a beam from a flashlight shining across a dark room. The beam is made of many photons traveling in a straight line. At the same time, light contains areas called electric fields and magnetic fields. These fields form wavelike patterns along light rays.

But light waves don't cause matter to vibrate the way sound waves do. Light waves can travel through empty space, with or without matter. And Huygens's ether does not exist.

No matter? No problem.

THE UNCHANGING UNIVERSE

How did the universe begin? That might be one of the oldest questions in history. Early humans told stories to explain how the world began. These stories usually involved a god creating the universe from nothing.

Aristotle had a different idea. He believed the universe had existed forever, was unchanging, and would always exist. Scientists who came after Aristotle agreed. As late as the early 1900s, many scientists thought the universe had always been the same size and always would be. German physicist Albert Einstein was one of these scientists.

Albert Einstein

Also in the early 1900s, inventors developed new, more powerful telescopes. They allowed scientists to see things beyond our solar system. Scientists learned more about the Milky Way **galaxy**. It contains hundreds of billions of stars and solar systems, including our own. Many scientists thought the entire universe was contained in the Milky Way.

galaxy: a vast system of stars, gas, dust, and other matter held together by gravity

In 1923, US astronomer Edwin Hubble spotted a "star" that was much farther away than the edge of the Milky Way. He soon realized it wasn't a star at all. It was another galaxy. But it was so far away that it looked like a distant star. Suddenly, the universe had gotten a lot bigger.

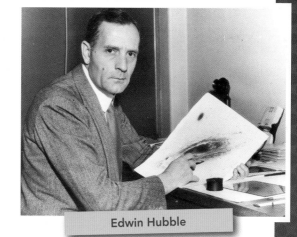

Edwin Hubble

And that wasn't all Hubble saw. He found other galaxies. By studying their light, he determined that all galaxies were moving away from one another. This discovery showed that the universe was expanding.

In the 1930s, Belgian astronomer Georges Lemaître reasoned that if the universe was expanding, it must have been smaller in the past. He figured that if we could travel back far enough in time, we would eventually reach a moment when all the matter in the universe was packed together into one very dense particle. Based on this idea, other scientists devised a theory called the big bang. They said the universe began when that particle expanded in a giant explosion.

Scientists think the big bang happened about fourteen billion years ago. What came before that, though, is anyone's guess!

SOURCE NOTES

10   *Journeys into the Moon, Several Planets and the Sun* (Philadelphia: Vollmer and Haggenmacher, 1837), 172.

12   H. G. Wells, "The War of the Worlds," *Project Gutenberg,* 1898, accessed December 1, 3012, http://www.gutenberg.org/files/36/36-h/36-h.htm.

12   National Aeronautics and Space Administration, "All about Mars: 1700s," *Mars Exploration Program,* accessed November 6, 2013, http://mars.nasa.gov/allaboutmars/mystique/history/1700/.

FURTHER INFORMATION

Bortz, Fred. *Seven Wonders of Space Technology.* Minneapolis: Twenty-First Century Books, 2011.
Read about improvements in space technology. Each new tool or technique helped people understand more about the universe.

Exploratorium
http://www.exploratorium.edu
At this website, a project of the Exploratorium science museum in San Francisco, California, you'll find information, activities, videos, and apps dealing with a wide variety of science topics, including physics and astronomy.

The Galileo Project
http://galileo.rice.edu
This website provides a wealth of information about the lives and work of Galileo Galilei and other scientists of his era. These scientists helped change our ideas about physics and astronomy.

Margles, Samantha. *Mythbusters Science Fair Book.* New York: Scholastic, 2011.
This book is packed with dozens of myth-busting science fair projects you can do at school or at home.

LERNER

SOURCE

Expand learning beyond the printed book. Download free, complementary educational resources for this book from our website, www.lernerresource.com.

Miller, Ron. *Recentering the Universe.* Minneapolis: Twenty-First Century Books, 2014.
In this book, follow the fascinating story of Nicolaus Copernicus, Johannes Kepler, Galileo Galilei, and Isaac Newton as they considered whether Earth orbited the sun.

Rowell, Rebecca. *Forces and Motion through Infographics.* Minneapolis: Lerner Publications, 2014.
The charts, maps, and illustrations in this book help explain key concepts about forces and motion.

Solar System Exploration
http://solarsystem.nasa.gov/index.cfm
This website from the National Aeronautics and Space Agency examines our solar system and our efforts to explore it.

Strange Science
http://science.discovery.com/strange-science
At this site by the Science Channel, you can explore science hoaxes, science feuds, science mistakes, and more. In addition to a treasure trove of fascinating information and photographs, this website includes many videos, activities, and interactive features.

Vogt, Gregory L. *Is There Life on Other Planets? And Other Questions about Space.* Minneapolis: Lerner Publications, 2010.
In this book, you can explore seventeen space-related statements to find out which ones are actually true.

Walker, Sally M. *Investigating Light.* Minneapolis: Lerner Publications, 2012.
The sun, lightbulbs, and flickering fires all bring light to our world. But have you ever watched light rays moving? Or seen how light rays reflect off objects? Now you can! Explore light with the fun experiments you'll find in this book.

Wandering Stars
http://www.nakedeyeplanets.com/movements.htm
Do you want to see exactly how the planets move against a background of stars? Are you curious why the skies look as they do from Earth? The diagrams and other information on this website will help you understand these difficult astronomical concepts.

YES. *Hoaxed! Fakes and Mistakes in the World of Science.* Tonawanda, NY: Kids Can Press, 2009.
This book uncovers and explains seventeen brilliantly bogus stories from the history of science.

INDEX

PHOTO ACKNOWLEDGMENTS

The images in this book are used with the permission of: © iStockphoto.com/uncle-rico, p. 2; © iStockphoto.com/Difydave, used throughout (star); © iStockphoto.com/loops7, used throughout (star); © Germanisches Nationalmuseum, Nuremberg, Germany/The Bridgeman Art Library, p. 4; © Universal History Archive/UIG/The Bridgeman Art Library, p. 5; © Science and Society/SuperStock, p. 6 (top); © DeAgostini/SuperStock, p. 6 (left); © James Steidl/Shutterstock.com, p. 6 (bottom); © iStockphoto.com/javarman3, p. 7; © iStockphoto.com/inhauscreative, pp. 8–9 (Jupiter); © iStockphoto.com/MarcelC, pp. 8–9 (Saturn); © Bettmann/CORBIS, p. 9 (top); © AISA/Courtesy Everett Collection, p. 9 (bottom); NASA/Solar Dynamics Observatory, p. 10 (top); National Maritime Museum/Courtesy Everett Collection, p. 10 (bottom); NASA and Erich Karkoschka, University of Arizona, p. 11 (Uranus); NASA/SDO/HMI, p. 11 (sun); Warner Brothers/Kobal Collection/Art Resource, NY, p. 12 (top); NASA/Goddard Space Flight Center Scientific Visualization Studio, p. 12 (bottom); © Detlev van Ravenswaay/Science Source, p. 13 (right); © broukoid/Shutterstock.com, p. 13 (left); © CVADRAT/Shutterstock.com, pp. 14–15 (Pluto); Lowell Observatory Archives/Wikimedia Commons, p. 14; AP Photo, p. 15 (top); © BSIP/Science Source, p. 15 (bottom); © Mike Agliolo/Science Source, p. 16 (top); © British Library Board. All rights reserved/The Bridgeman Art Library, p. 16 (bottom left); © iStockphoto.com/kimberrywood, pp. 16–17 (symbols); Wikimedia Commons (public domain), pp. 17, 19 (bottom), 25; © Andrew J Martinez/Science Source, p. 18 (left and right); © Okea/Dreamstime.com, pp. 18–19 (moon); © Somchai Som/Shutterstock.com, pp. 18–19 (moon); © Europhotos/Dreamstime.com, p. 19 (top); © Musee de la Tapisserie, Bayeux, France/with special authorization of the city of Bayeaux/The Bridgeman Art Library, p. 20; © VooDoo13/Shutterstock.com, pp. 20–21 (comet); © Science Source, pp. 21 (top right), 24, 26 (bottom left); © Paul D. Stewart/Science Source, p. 21 (bottom); © iStockphoto.com/Alexey Ivanov, pp. 22–23 (golf balls); © pterwort/Shutterstock.com, p. 22 (pin); © OZaiachin/Shutterstock.com, pp. 22–23 (bowling ball); NASA, p. 23; Private Collection/© Look and Learn/The Bridgeman Art Library, p. 22 (bottom); © iStockphoto.com/lumpynoodles, pp. 24–25 (molecules); © iStockphoto.com/dalton00, pp. 26–27 (light bulb); © iStockphoto.com/choness, p. 26 (top right); © The Print Collector/CORBIS, p. 27 (top); © iStockphoto.com/DeadDuck, p. 27 (bottom); © iStockphoto.com/jazle, p. 28 (top); Ferdinand Schmutzer/Wikimedia Commons (public domain), p. 28 (bottom); Hale Observatories, courtesy AIP Emilio Segre Visual Archives, p. 29. Front cover: © Ali Ender Birer/Dreamstime.com (Earth); © del.Monaco/Shutterstock.com (sky).